The Insatiable Cloud

How Wall Street &

Washington Broke Capitalism

From the series

Fire the Federal Government!
No.2

www.MAFarrellBooks.com

FIRST EDITION

Printed on acid-free paper

Library of Congress Cataloging-in-Publication Data has been applied for.

ISBN: 9781467989602

Books By
M. A. Farrell

Fact

Fire the Federal Government Series

No. 1 The Mustang States

No. 2 The Insatiable Cloud

Fiction
State of Mine
(A Political Thriller Trilogy)

State of Mine – Battle!

State of Mine - Rewrite

IN GOLD WE TRUST

A peoples' money is their reflection. If it be strong and respected, so too are they. If it be weak and debased, so too are the makers.
- Milton Bern
Professor of Economics

Secretary of the Treasury, Wyoming

From

STATE OF MINE - A Political Thriller Trilogy

PART I

THE PERPETRATORS

WHERE THE HECK IS OUR MONEY!

Washington has pumped TRILLIONS and TRILLIONS of dollars into our economy via deficit spending and Federal Reserve monetary policy. And the U.S. economy still has no legs.

Legs! What am I saying? The economy is flat on its face; prostrate.

We've printed all this money, indentured ourselves, our children and our children's children to generations of servitude (servicing just the interest on a staggering national debt). Yet the economy sputters. With all the money out there, the Fed should be trying to cool off economic activity.

So what's going on? Where did all the money go?

Well here's the answer: A hundred-thousand feet over our heads is a new kind of economy within which us 'Main Street-ers' are not allowed to compete. It's an ethereal economy, a phantom economy; a **Cloud economy**. And every day it competes with our real economy down here on *terra firma*.

And guess who wins the competition.

There are no angels on this cloud. In truth, the protesters on Wall Street would call these mercenaries-of-money the Devil.

For politeness, I prefer to call them *Casino Capitalists*. They make Saudi princes tossing dice in Monte Carlo look like back-alley craps throwers. They gamble with the largest stakes in history: our economy and our future. And when they come up with 'snake eyes,' hey, no problem.

You see, they maneuver their Cloud right over our nation's Capital as if it were a drive-thru McDonalds. When these guys eat through the entire Happy Meal of bailouts and stimuli, Washington turns on the fryers (i.e. printing presses) and, WHOOSH, all the moola is sucked right up into their insatiable cloud. McDonald's neon signs boast as having served billions of hamburgers. When Washington gets around to hanging out its sign, it will have to change 'burgers' to 'dollars' and 'billions' to 'trillions.'

If they were making reasonable bets on the real economy, all the debt our nation has racked-up *might* have been worth it. Then it would have created real wealth, and real jobs. But this isn't the case. Instead these guys and gals (can't leave the girls out) invented their own game by creating obscure 'assets' that no one really understands and represent nothing of real value.

It's kind of like using Monopoly money to buy those little, plastic hotels. They may demand real-world prices, but you can't sleep in them.

THE HEAT IS ON

The crowds filling Wall Street are on to something. They smell that The Street has done something with our money. And they want it back. It's starting to look like they might not wait much longer.

Things could heat up. And it could be bad for all of us.

Here are the three main groups 'Woodstocking' Wall Street. Group 'A' is people legitimately mad at Wall Street for eating up all our cash and producing no jobs. I call them the 'No-Bread-ers.' They want no more of our 'bread' (dough, moola, green stuff, dead presidents) going to Wall Street. They *do* want more bread in their wallets and bellies. These are Main Street-ers. I like this crowd.

Group 'B' is the progeny of the '60's hippies, looking to score some good stash, sing some bad songs and have an excuse to skip bathing. They have little interest in anything except a 'hip' party. I never liked this crowd.

Group 'C' is the Socialists. They know how to agitate, organize and bend the anger of the first group to their agenda. (They also know the second group is so stoned, it'll follow the crowd anywhere). Of course, the Socialists don't paint their name or intentions on signs. That would spoil the surprise ending.

No, they simply call themselves 'economic liberals,' just like the crowd in Washington D.C. This group is filled with dangerous people. They have a plan and a mission. It's to destroy Capitalism. **I hate this crowd**.

Wall Street can ignore the No-Bread-ers. Obama can chide them; then spur them on, all in the same press conference. But both Washington and The Street had better pay heed. Main Street is angry enough to listen to group 'C' (Socialists). And people without jobs (and no hope of one in the near future) tend to get vicious. Put groups A & C together (with B strumming background) and we could have a very un-merry Christmas.

To the No-Bread-ers I say that I'm fuming about the condition of our economy as well. But, to date, I have not heard concrete solutions from your camp. Therefore I write this book for you and for all Main Street-ers rooting you on. There's a game plan contained within this short book that will disarm Wall Street, allow us to take back our country and save Capitalism.

A TOUGH CROWD

I only hope that we can focus the wrath of Group A on the right targets before the 'economic liberals' (Socialists) turn their heads. This economy is ready for the real plummet unless we can quickly fix what's wrong.

Don't believe economists. We aren't about to 'double-dip' into recession. We have a few years of so-called 'recovery' before taking a triple gainer off the high dive right into a '9.5' depression (no multiplying for 'difficulty' because the Fed is making it so easy). But it won't be the Great Depression of the 1930's when dollars were scarce and 25 cents bought the blue-plate special. No, it's going to be like Germany's depression of the 1920's: hyperinflation. Then it took 127 Billion Marks (yes, *Billion* with a capital 'B') to buy a loaf of bread. Thank God they had Billion Mark notes (seriously). Otherwise you'd need a wheelbarrow instead of a wallet.

Anyone have change for a billion?

Here's a scary fact. The No-Bread-ers *are not* going to stand in soup lines for ten years waiting for the next depression to end. They're going to riot in the streets and then start shooting. Socialists, and their Communist brethren, will make sure of this.

(Know the difference between a Socialist and a Communist? The Socialist dances in the street after gaining complete control of the economy and society. Then the Communist shoots him in the head and takes power. HA!...that one always cracks me up).

Fortunately (or unfortunately) we will not have a Franklin-Roosevelt-type on the radio calming our frustrations and fears with 'Fireside Chats.' (There's a lot better programming to choose from today). Roosevelt realized he was facing a potential revolution and the resulting overturn of our political structure. There were protests in the street, just like now. Capitalism was demonized (borrowing your word, Barak) as having failed. The Socialists sensed that their opportunity to take over was near. And the Commie's were polishing finger prints off their NKVD Nagants (that's a pistol used by nasty Russians). Roosevelt grasped the threatening lure of the siren's (a.k.a. Socialist) call to a people desperate for jobs, food and hope; the No-Bread-ers. So he chose the absolutely wrong path.

He did not fix the Federal Reserve's mismanagement of the money supply. Instead he listened to 'flaming' liberals like John Canadian Socialist Galbraith and his poison-pen pal across the pond, John English Socialist Keynes. Roosevelt bypassed the Fed and enshrined deficit spending as a legitimate monetary policy. However, deficit spending is *not* a legitimate tool for monetary policy. It is debt, pure and simple. When the government spends money, it is an expense, not an investment. And when government competes with Capitalism for capital, Capitalism loses; so does the economy, and so too society. Government 'make work' programs are just another expense borne by the private sector. It doesn't create lasting jobs. It creates *the dole.* Even Rome didn't last on this system.

Deficit spending is a weapon of Socialists and Communists. It's the method by which these ideologies take over an economy. When the economic system collapses (because it can't compete with government debt) Socialists salivate. They declare the failure of Capitalism and push for complete government take-over of the economy (with the Commies in the wings, loading their Nagants).

Government spending for WWII **did not** end Roosevelt's depression, as liberals love to tout. What it did was to create a four-year hiatus filled by government jobs (military and war production) and government spending. Inflation wasn't a big concern because there was little to buy (due to rationing) and the government sopped up extra cash (in the form of War Bonds). After the war, the economy dipped downward and government fretted that the depression was returning. What really ended the depression was an increased money supply and government spending aimed at technological gains ('the future is plastics, my boy, PLASTICS!). These technological advances assisted Capitalism well, filling pent-up consumer demand (all those returning, love-starved GI's creating us 'Baby Boomers').

What WW II *did* create was a generation disciplined by war, with a renewed sense of national pride and patriotism. Capitalism served well this generation to such extent that patriotism and Capitalism fused. With the rise of the Cold War, the mesh of these two became even stronger in face of our newest enemy: Communism (translated: Russian missiles pointing at us). America patriotically adopted Capitalism. Capitalism ranked with mom, apple pie and the flag.

Americans created a CONTRACT WITH CAPITALISM. And here's the essence of the Contract: Serve us and we'll serve you.

The Contract worked, for twenty-five years. And then one branch of Capitalism, in cahoots with Washington D.C., broke it.

Creation Capitalism

I am a Creation capitalist. I get my kicks, satisfaction (and money) creating and growing a company. When things go right, it's thrilling. Not only do I use my God-given talents to make a lot of money, but I gain respect for building something of worth to me, the people I hire and the customers I serve. I also take pride that I've added to the wealth of our nation. You may call me corny or insincere, but cross-my-heart, I mean it. Bill Gates and Steve Jobs (sadly deceased) strode the world as revered icons of Capitalism. Above the adulation is their inner satisfaction of building something worthy to society; a corporation to outlast their too-short stay in this world. How would you feel to leave Microsoft or Apple as your legacy? (I know, just give you their money instead; you cynic). It is difficult to describe the feeling of pride each time your product or service is purchased. Every sales unit is a vote by society, and you are the winner! (Like when you bought this book!). Ending a year with high profits is the equivalent of spiking the football in the end zone. Okay, it's egocentric. Creation Capitalists possess enormous egos that allow us to continue the battle long after others give up. We prefer the term *tenacity*, but it's ego.

Another name for Creation Capitalists is *entrepreneurs*.   We bring wealth and jobs to society. It's a combination of employees, markets and customers. In other words, it's about *people*. It's about *Main Street.*

Creation Capitalism alone holds the promise of improvement and advancement for all. Even its loudest enemy, Communism, unknowingly acknowledges this.

Following are two statements from Karl Marx. It seems strange for a Capitalist to quote the founder of Communism. But, as Tsun Tsu (or Ronald McDonald) said: knowing your enemy's thoughts and letting his own words pull his pants down is really cool.

Marx's ideology may have partially developed from a true empathy for working conditions; conditions unique to his time. (Yes, they were third world, sweat shop conditions. But, hey, we Capitalists were just getting started). There were so many workers escaping even-worse squalor out in the feudalistic countryside, competition for limited jobs was ferocious. Wages and working conditions reflected it. (We're businessmen after all, not Mother Teresa). But remember this: these workers (*nee* peasants) must have thought it was a heck of a lot better than being whipped by the Estate Manager, or plowing mud behind a defecating ox or shoveling feces out of thatched-roof hovels.

What I hear through Marx and his writings is the tantrum of a spoiled kid revolting against the wealth he enjoyed growing up. (Sounds like that reality series wherein worthless, rich brats, sit in Daddy's Ferrari, swilling Daddy's single-malt scotch, and quote Nietzsche while staring into the abyss, stoned). Marx was a rebel with a clause. And Daddy's Capitalism was his target.

Note to Father Marx: You should have spanked the kid. Instead, you turned him and his whacky ideas loose on humanity.

Here's the first quote:

> *History calls those men the greatest who*
> *have ennobled themselves by working for the*
> *common good; experience acclaims as*
> *happiest the man who has made the greatest*
> *number of people happy.*

Marx, Letter to His Father (1837)

Karl, I ask you one question. Who brought more 'good' and 'happiness' to this world? You, with your gray hopelessness and grinding poverty of Communism? You with the human slaughter and imprisonment of millions? Or your father and his ilk creating jobs that lured millions from the pestilence, poverty and ignorance of their former lives as peasants? In the two largest experiments of Communism (Russia & China), the *workers' paradise* became hell on earth. It's only since the former Communist monolith turned to Capitalism that their people have begun to live.

Another quote from Marx:

> *Capital is money: Capital is commodities. ...*
> *Because it is value, it has acquired the occult*
> *quality of being able to add value to itself. It*
> *brings forth living offspring, or, at the least,*
> *lays golden eggs.*

Marx, *Capital*, Volume I, Chapter 4 (1867)

Watch it, Karl. Daddy's Capitalism is showing! In this one statement Marx shows the impracticability of Communism. It states that Capitalism keeps adding value to itself (and, therefore, society), and that it lays the *golden eggs* (wealth). Yet Marx thinks that the eggs will continue to be laid even when Capitalists are in chains. After all, Communism is the *dictatorship of the proletariat.* Do you really think Creation Capitalists would dedicate their lives and treasure to toiling for a society that promised no wealth? No social status? No political inclusion? No freedom? Creation Capitalism *requires* freedom, Mr. Marx. No freedom, no eggs.

What a foolish man.

Creation Capitalism is *the tide that raises all boats.* It alone has been responsible for the greatest wealth-creation of a nation in history (empires stole their wealth from others), the largest food abundance, the highest living standards, the greatest increase in education of the masses, the most rapid advances in science and medicine, the longest life-span, the lowest child mortality rate and the grandest outbreak of individual liberty in history.

And it was first to put a man in outer-space using private capital. (Thank you, Bert & Richard).

So what went wrong? Why are we in the economic mess we struggle with today?

Remember the rising tide and the boats? Well, someone has been drilling holes in the bottom of everyone else's boat, except their own.

Casino Capitalists
(A.K.A. 'The Money Guys')

There is another branch of Capitalism other than Creation Capitalists. It's called Casino Capitalists. The two branches of Capitalism developed in tandem, for they require each other. It is a symbiotic relationship.

Creation Capitalism is pure alchemy. It turns money into jobs and wealth. But it does need the money first. For this, it often turns to the Money branch of the Capitalist tree. In the beginning of Capitalism, providers of capital (for a financial return) were referred to as money-lenders. Later they became money brokers. Then they became bankers. Then they became investment bankers. Then they became Casino Capitalists. (These guys morphed more than a *Transformer*).

Creation Capitalists pretty much followed the same model with which they started: develop an idea for a winning product or service; pitch the idea to Money Capitalists in order to get a loan; hire workers (create jobs); produce the product or service; receive profits from sales; pay off the original loan; do it all over again in order to keep the company growing; reap (hopefully) expanding profits. The products and services produced may have become more spectacular, but the process remains the same.

This is not true of Casino Capitalists.

Listen up, Pilgrim. This is important: CASINO CAPITALISTS MAKE MONEY FROM MONEY. And they make huge, risky bets in order to make that money. Hence the term CASINO CAPITALISTS (too subtle?) They do not create goods and services. They do not create jobs. They are sharks. And these big sharks spawn little protégé sharks, swimming out of Ivy Leagues.

Casino Capitalists started as money lenders (remember the guys Jesus got physical with in the Temple?) Usually, money lenders loaned *their* money (not OPM – Other People's Money). Leary of hucksters, ideas with little or no chance of success, or persons of turpitude, money lenders were beyond conservative. The term *tight-fisted* was invented for this group. The reputation accompanied them throughout history. Even as they became modern bankers, they wore terms such as 'conservative' and 'staid' with pride. And speaking of 'wearing', even their dress was conservative: Brooks Brothers three-piece suits, white shirt, plain tie and wing-tipped shoes. Flashiness of dress reflected lack of stability, lack of judgment and lack of maturity. Flashiness wasn't good marketing to people trusting their money to these guys. Besides, flashiness cost too much. And, remember, these guys were skinflints.

(Today, this crowd is wearing Savile Row suits, Armani shirts, Berluti Rapiécés Reprisés shoes and Patek Philippe watches. Hmmmm....wonder what changed?)

Such conservatism of the original Money Capitalists reflected in their lending practices. Other people's money was treated as their own. They didn't quantify, categorize or chart *risk* (as they do today) because *risk-avoidance* was their goal. *Risk-aversion* was their faith. The old adage applied: "Bankers only lend money to those that show they don't need it."

Then it all changed.

I cannot exactly pinpoint when Money Capitalists turned Casino Capitalists. However, the symbolic rise of Casino Capitalists can be personified in one man: Michael Robert Milken. During the 1970's through the 1980's Milken was into high-yield finance. He was a mover and shaker, able to raise a million dollars for a customer in the span of one hour on the phone. He financed casinos in Las Vegas, with Steve Wynn becoming a major customer (maybe this is where the handle *Casino* came from?). He was a major fund-raiser for the leveraged-buy-outs (LBOs) and 'green mailers' during the 1980's. Milken ran the high-yield department for a struggling investment bank with a history of ups-downs and mergers: Drexel Burnham Lambert (as it eventually came to rest). Drexel had only two clients in 1970 and not a lot to lose. So it let loose Milken to run its high-yield department. High yields meant high returns. It also meant high risk, because the bonds he bought and sold were rated low, low, low. His funds created a new industry term: *junk bonds* and Milken was knighted *Junk Bond King.*

Here's the part that somehow escapes Casino Capitalist (and most gamblers): HIGH RISK CAN TRANSLATE INTO HIGH LOSES!

And that's what happened when it all crashed in 1990; Drexel went bankrupt; investors lost hundreds of millions of dollars; and Milken (after several appeals) went to jail, pleading guilty to six counts of SEC violations. (He was 'betrayed' by a fellow-traveler in the RISK world, Ivan Boesky. What a great group of guys).

To this day, Milken is respected by many on Wall Street as an 'innovator' and a winner. Though he was banned for life from the securities industry, in 2010 *Forbes* still listed him as the 488th richest person in the world. Apparently his mega losses had little impact on his *personal* bank account. He even has a Charity in his name (wonder what it invests in?) Oh, well, win some, lose some. It wasn't his money anyway. That, apparently, was invested in something safe.

Many of Milken's circumventions of SEC rules, though not all illegal, were certainly not within bounds of SEC attempts at reducing risk. This, as much as the returns he made, captured the imagination of The Street and of the up-and-coming baby sharks that would soon have control over a significant portion of our nation's capital.

(Hmmm, I wonder where Oliver Stone got his inspiration for Gordon Gekko?. I wonder how many Bud Fox's learned, admired and assimilated Milken's methods along with his moral standards?)

Every major investment house incorporated a high yield department. Wall Street had learned the wrong lessons: First, high risk is profitable. Second: high risk is dangerous…but so what? It's not our money. Third: create your own high risk niche. Heck, create your own financial instruments. The Street calls it 'innovation.'

And, boy, did Wall Street innovate. They created Credit derivatives. And then they created Credit derivatives of Credit derivatives. *Derivative* means its value is based on (or *derived* from) another financial instrument. And that financial instrument is a debt owed by someone, supposedly secured by an asset sitting around somewhere under the title 'anonymous.'

Wanna buy one? Quick! Give me your money before I change my mind!

I'm not saying all derivatives are a bad thing. Some derivatives have been around for ages and actually 'smooth-out' market swings. Some provide great service to business and even to governments. But these derivatives are based on real, tangible *assets*. They aren't based on *Credit* instruments.

Take for example Forward Fx – foreign exchange – contracts. If a business sells internationally and receives foreign currency from its sale of products or services, it might wish to escape the potential swings of currency valuations in order to present a stable selling-price to its international customer. So it purchases a Forward Fx contract. This means it books a future purchase of foreign currency for future delivery, hence the 'Forward.' It's based on a discount from the spot market (today's price). The company can now set its price level in the currency of its customer for whatever number of months in the future.

An Fx contract is not a Credit derivative. It derives its value from a real asset; in this case the actual currency to be delivered, or made available in the future. Fx contracts are important to importers and exporters because they do business in different currencies. Buying Forward Fx contracts provides price and profit stability longer range.

Another example of a beneficial (and non-Credit) derivative is a Commodity Future. This is very similar to a Forward Fx contract except the underlying asset is a commodity instead of a currency. Commodities can be oil, coal, precious metals, orange juice, pork bellies, or beef and lamb. A supplier smoothes out swings in annual production and profit by offering some or all of a commodity for delivery in the future at a fixed price today. This way a sale is already guaranteed for a product that might not yet have been made (or ripened, grown or pumped). For some commodities, such as oil, the futures market sets the world price.

To emphasize that a Commodities derivative is backed by a real asset, just don't sell one you've bought. In three months (or six, or whatever time limit of the instrument), you will get a phone call as to where you want the truck-load of pork bellies dumped. Better have a real big refrigerator on hand.

(By the way, ever wonder why traders sell pork bellies? I did, for a long time. It's what rashers of bacon are carved from. I guess that speaks volumes as to how much we really don't watch our cholesterol. You can slip in that little fact at your next cocktail party, or trivia game).

These financial instruments represent real assets and assist in the production of future goods. It's a pre-sell that lets the producer know how much to produce. It is a means to avoid over-production. Although these instruments carry the stigma of being derivatives, they are vital to an economy's long range stability.

But when you get into bundled Credit derivatives or derivatives of Credit derivatives, financial instruments of this nature become dangerous. They can be several steps away from the loan they supposedly represent, and miles from the asset securing the loan. And because financial instruments take on a life, (valuation) all their own, multiple instruments representing a single asset often exceed the value of the original asset by several multiples.

To make that last sentence more understandable, think of this example: Joe buys a car worth $30k and Joe gets a loan from the car maker for the entire $30k (YES FOLKS, I'M TALKING ZERO DOWN AND ZERO PERCENT INTEREST! For the next 48 hours). The car company sells the loan off to a financial institution that bundles Joe's car loan with a thousand other car loans into a new financial instrument we shall call LAL's - Lousy Auto Loans. See I can name it whatever I want because I created this new, INNOVATIVE financial instrument.
Then the financial institution sells its invented instrument to another financial company that ships it offshore to be sliced into *tranches*, strips out I/O coupons, creates layers and, just for chuckles, bundles some of these goodies into another derivative and sells that to another financial institution. (All of these terms are explained just a few pages away. Hang in there).

Joe's original loan is only a miniscule fraction of the value of the derivative bond (Yep, these are classified as bonds. But it ain't Granpa's old AT&T bonds anymore). Yet if you add up all the slices and dices, layers and coupons, tranches and franches (my fun), the total portion representing Joe's loan is worth (pre 2007) $60k, TWICE THE VALUE OF THE ORIGINAL LOAN that the bond was based upon!

Wait! There's more (this gets wackier and wackier).

Now, we all know Joe's car dropped in value the day it left the lot. Let's say it was of Japanese manufacturer, so it only depreciated 20%. The underlying asset is now only worth $24k (securing $60k in derivatives).

But it's okay, because the loan is actually backed up by Joe's promise (faith and credit) to pay off the loan.

Unfortunately, when everything collapsed in 2007, Joe lost his job a year later. He couldn't continue to make the car payment. So the original financial institution repossessed the car. They sold it at wholesale auction for $15K. Now the financial institution doesn't really own the loan anymore (even though they have papers that say they do), so they try to figure out where the money goes. If they are somewhat legit (big gamble on that one), they forward the money to the institution that bought the original derivative. But that institution (who did the slicing, dicing, etc.) really has no idea who owns

Joe's loan, so they make an accounting entry and then use the money for some other riskier investment. If, someday, someone comes forward asking for their one-hundredth-thousandth slice of the money, the institution finds some way to show that the loan had lost all value; probably through some sort of holding/handling/compounded/slice-and-diced fees. If anyone yells 'foul,' the financial institution smiles and says, "We made an accounting entry. We did nothing wrong. See ya in court."

So when the music stopped in 2007, not only were these credit derivatives previously over-valued by 200% to 400%, no one could even find the original assets they were based upon.

The original boys peddling this stuff were real slick. I've got to take my hat off to them. To think of an entire nation shafted. Oooooo.... It gives me goose bumps.

Credit derivatives and derivatives of Credit derivatives are mazes of potential confusion, obfuscation and even corruption; layer upon worthless layer of credit inflation that can burst. They are proven to be harmful to an economy, yet they still exist and are traded today. The crisis of 2007 was spurred on by these instruments. They were what horn-swoggled individuals and stupid financial institutions held when the last credit bubble burst.

The first *innovators* out of the shoot were the young sharks at JP Morgan. Their contribution was the CDS, or Credit Default Swap, or just 'swap.' It spread out risk in that it 'swapped' debt owed the bank by one corporation to another corporation. The bank still remained the loan guarantor and payment collector for the CDS buyer. However, it allowed them to put forth the case that the loan was now 'off the books' and should not be used within calculations determining their reserve requirements. Less reserve requirement means more money to loan out, providing more return to the bank. But lower reserves mean lowering the ability of banks to withstand financial assaults during major downturns. The success of these instruments turned Jamie Dimon's young sharks into rock stars within the financial world (Mr. Dimon is CEO of JP Morgan Chase Bank). And their model was adopted by the industry. The race was on.

What was so egregious about JP Morgan's methods was not just the initial instrument. (Warren Buffet calls Swaps "Dangerous and anti-social." I like Mr. Buffet for a whole lot of reasons). It was, first, the obvious attempt at circumventing rules that maintain some semblance of solvency to our banking system in order to weather economic storms. Second is the infrastructure for these instruments: The *BISTRO* - Broad Index Secured Trust Offering - was invented as an off-shore (again, circumvention) method to take financial instruments and slice them into pieces (*tranches*). Morgan even refers to these as *synthetic securitisations* [sic..*securitizations*].

I can only guess at the meaning of this catchy phrase. Let's see, something from nature is 'natural' and something man-made is 'synthetic.' So whatever these instruments are, they aren't natural. Okay, I buy that. Maybe this is Morgan's attempt at 'truth-in-investing.'

Here's another fun detail about the Bistro. This is a quote from JP Morgan:

> *In transactions executed to date, investors know the specific names and amounts of exposures comprising the BISTRO portfolio at issue.* [Gosh, that sounds good]. *Banking secrecy laws (particularly in Europe), however, mean that it can be necessary to restrict disclosure of the underlying names…*

That sounds a little risky, don't you think? I kind of like knowing in whom I've invested. I'm just funny that way.

So now we have off-shore slicing, dicing and layering of these anonymous instruments. And JP Morgan wasn't going to be left alone to have all this fun. No siree. Every financial institution wanted in on this. The money was just too easy and sloughing off risk onto unsophisticated buyers was even juicier. The dam burst.

Just in CDSs, you have the following derivations: Dynamic credit swap or credit intermediation swap, Substitution option, Two-name exposure, Total (rate of) return swap, First-to-default swap and Credit spread option.

Here's another sample of one of the derivatives that did some real damage in the last collapse, CDOs – Collateralized Debt Obligations. Its spawn includes: CLOs, CBOs, CSOs, SFCDOs, CRE CDOs, CIOs, CDO-Squared, and (one of my favorites) CDO^n. (Is that a *hosing* to the nth degree, or just leaving room for a new bomb not yet thought of?).

And here's the real winner, the one that accompanied the housing collapse and almost brought down the world-wide financial system, the CMO – Collateralized Mortgage Obligation – and its spawn: Z bonds, TAC bonds, PAC bonds, VADM, NAS, and NASequential. And the best part is that you can slice them up many different ways (tranches): We can opt for Credit tranches, Prepayment tranches Parallel tranches, Sequential tranches, or (another one of my favorites) Coupons (strips). In this category there are IO/discount fixed rate pairs, PO/premium fixed rate pairs, IO/PO pair, or (hold the mayo) just IO pair and PO pair. I won't bore you with Inverse IOs, TTIBs, Digital TTIBs/Superfloaters, and 'mountain' bonds, WAC IOs and WAC POs. (Oops, too late).

What's the point of this mind-numbing list? Here it is: No one really knows exactly how these things work, in what form they should be owned, how to price them or how to establish their worth. Below is JP Morgan's explanation of the benefit of Swap short sales. Have your aspirin bottle handy:

Second, credit derivatives are the first mechanism via which short sales of credit instruments can be executed with any reasonable liquidity and without the risk of a short squeeze. It is more or less impossible to short-sell a bank loan, but the economics of a short position can be achieved synthetically by purchasing credit protection using a credit derivative. This allows the user to reverse the "skewed" profile of credit risk (whereby one earns a small premium for the risk of a large loss) and instead pay a small premium for the possibility of a large gain upon credit deterioration. Consequently, portfolio managers can short specific credits or a broad index of credits, either as a hedge of existing exposures or simply to profit from a negative credit view. Similarly, the possibility of short sales opens up a wealth of arbitrage opportunities. Global credit markets today display discrepancies in the pricing of the same credit risk across different asset classes, maturities, rating cohorts, time zones, currencies, and so on. These discrepancies persist because arbitrageurs

*have traditionally been unable to purchase
cheap obligations against shorting expensive
ones to extract arbitrage profits. As credit
derivative liquidity improves, banks,
borrowers, and other credit players will exploit
such opportunities, just as the evolution of
interest rate derivatives first prompted cross-
market interest rate arbitrage activity in the
1980s. The natural consequence of this is, of
course, that credit pricing discrepancies will
gradually disappear as credit markets
become more efficient.*

Efficient? They mean *Obscure.* Did you get any of
the above? No? Why, that's as clear as mud! Tell
you what, first person that makes sense of that
paragraph in two sentences of Standard English, I'll
send them my next book, free.

What's the point?... 'Precisely', I answer. What *is* the
point of having all these financial instruments that no
one understands; that *have* caused and *will* cause
future financial disasters? The answer: to make
money from all the excess cash the Federal Reserve
has pumped into the banking system along with all
the profits derived from deficit spending by Congress
(and approved by the President).

Let these facts sit on your brain and germinate for a
moment. In 1835, Andrew Jackson paid off our
national debt. It was ZERO, zilch, nada when he left
office. Since 1835 to 1982 we, as a nation, have

accumulated for the intervening 147 years a *total* of one-trillion dollars in debt. Nothing to applaud, but not totally terrible for fighting two world wars, a bunch of smaller wars, saving the Free World from communism, along with deficit spending for eight recessions and one huge depression.

Yet, in the last three years we have added over ONE TRILLION DOLLARS EACH AND EVERY YEAR! Our national debt now stands at FIFTEEN TRILLION DOLLARS and will, conservatively, reach TWENTY-TWO TRILLION DOLLARS in the next ten years. This is an enormous amount of money. And just paying the interest on it will, very soon, consume our entire Federal budget.

So our economy staggers along, trying not to slide into another recession or, worse, a depression. There are no new jobs being created. Small businesses cannot get loans from banks, let alone the SBA – Small Business Administration. The largest corporations are floating bonds of enormous amounts at generous yields. They are doing this because they know the surge in interest rates (due to the Fed's increased money pumping) is just around the corner. Yet the bond market isn't rushing to buy them because they also know what's around the corner... BIG INFLATION!

We have mortgaged our future, our children's future and their children's future by continuing to engage in massive Federal spending that's supposed to rebuild our economy. SO WHERE'S ALL OUR MONEY?!

Like I told you at the beginning, it's been sucked up by another economy; a **Cloud economy**. And it's swirling around up there in these financial instruments, derivatives. They are so far removed from real assets that they only have value of what traders say they have. There is no intrinsic value to these dangerous pieces of paper. They can go up in smoke any second. They already did in 2007!

But can these financial instruments really absorb this amount of money? We're talking about TRILLIONS of dollars. Nobody could create something out of thin air that others would plow TRILLIONS into…could they? I'm afraid so. Here's another gem from JP Morgan:

> *Averaging $25 to $50 million per transaction, they range in size from a few million to billions of dollars. Reference Entities may be drawn from a wide universe including sovereigns, semi-governments, financial institutions, and all other investment or sub-investment grade corporates.*

Governments, financial institutions and large corporations are dealing in thousands of these instruments every day. And this quote is restricted to JP Morgan's Credit Default Swaps only. Add in all the other financial instruments out there, and all the other financial institutions floating in this **Cloud**

economy, and you can see who and what gobbled up the indebted money that we are on the hook for, but from which we have received no value. Not only are banks making more money this way, they don't have to deal with the headaches of running a *real* bank. All those pesky customers, credit checks, ratio calculations, paper shuffling, and collecting loan payments. It must be exhausting to those poor banker people. If you think I'm making this up, I offer the following JP Morgan quote:

> *To illustrate, bank loans have not traditionally appealed as an asset class to hedge funds and other nonbank institutional investors for at least two reasons: first, because of the administrative burden of assigning and servicing loans; and second, because of the absence of a repo market. Without the ability to finance investments in bank loans on a secured basis via some form of repo market, the return on capital offered by bank loans has been unattractive to institutions that do not enjoy access to unsecured financing.*

My teeth implants fell out at this statement. (Not really, I can't afford implants in this economy). Let me paraphrase the above, "We, the banking industry, give out loans at lousy spreads. So hedge funds don't want to include them in their high-yield (a.k.a., high-risk) portfolio. This means, as a bank we are stuck with bank loans. And this depresses our stock price and pisses-off our shareholders. But, through the use of derivatives, we can dump our stupid loans on hedge funds and then put our money into something with real return: other risky derivatives."

Here's their point truncated: Screw the national economy and screw the American public. We will use our money [sic...the nation's capital] any way we want.

If you think I made up these JP Morgan quotes, or took them out of context, please go to:

http://www.investinginbonds.com/assets/files/Intro_to Credit_Derivatives.pdf

If I were Jamie Dimon, I would take this site down as fast as possible. If this occurs and you can't find it, the complete document is available at my website:

www.firethefederalgovernment.com

In all of this, the part most scary is what our financial institutions are investing *our national capital* within. Americans know that derivatives were a major cause of the collapse starting in 2007. I would bet most of you reading this presumed that something has been done to eliminate or control these instruments of doom. I am sorry to be the bearer of bad news. Yes, there has been new laws enacted (Dodd-Franks, 2010), but they are inadequate to correct the problems. It's much as using a Band-Aid to stem the bleeding of a severed artery. Meanwhile, derivatives are morphing and spawning every day and more money than ever is finding its way into these instruments, not into our economy.

Another exciting point that will give you acid indigestion: derivatives can be (and usually are) bought on credit (margin) and somebody is loaning the money. Whether our financial institutions are investing in these directly or providing loans to those that are, the results become the same: a catastrophe waiting to happen.

Every downturn, recession or depression in our nation's modern history was caused by a credit collapse. And each credit bubble was caused by too much money in the economy chasing riskier and riskier investments…on credit. The larger the bubble, the larger the burst, the further the economy falls and the longer it takes for recovery. We are building up the largest credit bubble in history. When (not *if*) it bursts, we will be unable to spend our way out like we have in the past. We are a debtor nation. To print more money means we have to sell more Treasury bonds. And with our declining credit rating, there will be no buyers. If we just print the money and distribute it (which I think the Fed will do), we will have roaring inflation. It will result in an inflation-driven depression.

The Casino Capitalists are going down, and taking the rest of us with them. But I'm sure they've socked away enough money to enjoy a long depression (unless they're in jail). Obviously Michael Milken did. It's not their money they're losing anyway. All they worry about is the timing of their escape. They are fully aware of the risk at which they have put this country. Just look at the contributors and the publisher on the title page of JP Morgan's pamphlet:

THE J.P. MORGAN GUIDE

TO CREDIT DERIVATIVES

With Contributions from the **RiskMetrics** Group

Published by **Risk**

Sure makes me all warm and fuzzy to know they're handling our nation's capital. All of Wall Street keeps rolling the dice until it comes up snake eyes. The most they have to lose is their job. The rest of us may lose our country.

And here's a most startling fact: "the top six [SIX] banks…hold assets that equal almost 65% [SIXTY-FIVE PERCENT!] of America's GDP." (*Time* magazine, Dec. 2011). You don't think these institutions have their hands around our collective…throats? I'm not just picking on JP Morgan Chase. They are just one of the six. But all have their high-yield departments. (My capitalizations in brackets for emphasis. It's the only way an author can yell).

I leave this section with a final quote from the Morgan pamphlet:

However, five years hence, commentators will look back to the birth of the credit derivative market as a watershed development for bank credit risk management practice. Simply put, credit derivatives are fundamentally changing the way banks price, manage, transact, originate, distribute, and account for credit risk.

Not much to disagree with here, except the outcome.

PART II
THE CRIMES

What Is The Capitalist Contract?

I said earlier that, after World War II, Capitalists and America had formed a contract of mutual benefit: serve us and we will serve you. As with any Contract, there are at least two parties involved and the responsibilities are spelled out. The two sides in this Contract are Society and Capitalism. Following is the responsibility of Capitalism to provide Society, and how the Casino Capitalists and Washington D.C. broke the Contract.

Financial Stewardship

What is meant by 'financial stewardship' is how strong Washington D.C. maintains our dollar and our economy and how effectively it spends our money. As of now, they could not have done worse. The dollar is collapsing daily. How is Wall Street involved in this governmental task? Of the last 28 Secretaries of the Treasury, twenty were either from large corporations or from the banking sector. The last one (Paulson) and the current one (Geithner) are from Wall Street firms.

The Federal Reserve is run by bankers (with a few economists thrown in for laughs).

Casino Capitalists are some of the largest contributors to our national political campaigns. And with the Supreme Court's recent ruling that allows corporations to contribute whatever amount they choose to political campaigns, this influence is even greater.

We give Casino Capitalists access to our political system and rely upon them to assist in governmental steering of the economy. It is implied that society has placed a large degree of faith within Casino Capitalists to provide our nation with financial stewardship.

Instead, the Casino Capitalists have used influence to chip-away and finally bring down the *Glass-Steagall Act* which had split banking into two distinct camps: regular deposit/loan banking and investment banking. The Act was in response to the 1929 Wall Street collapse (a.k.a. credit bubble burst) that began the Great Depression. Casino Capitalists posing as conservative bankers used relationship-banking to peddle unsuspecting customers high risk and even bundled, bad loans. *Glass-Steagall* also prevented banks from dealing in high risk instruments. That was left to the investment side. But, alas, no more.

We expect financial stewardship from the Casino Capitalists. Yet the banking industry is one of the highest leveraged and deepest in debt of most major corporations. Remember this fact: financial institutions do not just invest its customers' money. It invests money it borrows from other banks. In 2007, this was a major problem. With so much greater return in high risk derivatives, financial institutions not only created and sold them, they held them for themselves (caught drinking their own Kool-Aid). And a large amount of the derivatives were bought with money loaned by other financial institutions. In financial terms, this is called 'leverage.' When leverage is high in a corporation, banks shake their heads at requests for loans. However, financial institutions prior to 2007 *bragged* about their leverage. Wall Street averaged between 40:1 and 50:1. This translates thusly: for every one dollar of assets the institution owned, they had *borrowed* forty to fifty dollars! For every ONE MILLION DOLLARS they had listed as 'assets,' they had BORROWED FORTY TO FIFTY MILLION DOLLARS! Is there any question why, when the economy took a dive, the entire financial system of the Western World was brought to the brink of default? Banks, investment houses, even insurance companies (remember AIG?) couldn't repay their loans to each other because they couldn't sell those 'assets' their money was tied up in. The 'assets' were derivatives. Because of their complexity and anonymity of what was contained within, no one in their right mind would touch these financial instruments. That is why they became labeled as TOXIC!

And guess where a large amount of our financial gift (a.k.a. bailout, Stimuli, TARP, QE1~QE?; however you want to refer to it) was applied by these institutions. That's right, to loan more money to each other and to buy more derivatives. A good chunk was used to bolster shareholder value by buying back their own stock. And a nice slice was paid in bonuses to upper management of these failed institutions. BONUSES FOR FAILURE! (Where do I apply?).

Here we thought it was for banks to loan to Creation Capitalists in order to jump-start the economy and restore jobs. Silly us.

And here's some more cheery (chary?) news. Financial institutions have not reduced their leverage ratios if we apply a true accounting method. The reason is that they still have those toxic 'assets' in inventory and they still appear as 'assets' on their balance sheet. They are valued at what the banks *paid* for them, not what they could *sell* them for on the open market. If we forced them to 'minus' out these derivatives from their leverage calculations, Triple Ought on the roulette table would look a conservative investment.

Obviously this is not Financial Stewardship. This is Financial *Skewered-Ship*. And our nation's wealth is the meat on the shish kabob. So the Casino Capitalists have definitely broken this clause of the Contract.

National wealth & job creation

The prior section addressed this point. I add to this an additional thought; *ONLY CREATION CAPITALISTS CAN CREATE NATIONAL WEALTH AND LONG-LASTING JOBS.* This is not in the purview or abilities of Casino Capitalists or Washington D.C. Wealth is measured by goods and services produced and sold (GDP), plus a nation's accumulated foreign currencies and gold (representative of past goods and services produced and sold). Creation Capitalists can't create or expand companies (that provide jobs) without the fuel from Casino Capitalists. But this latter crowd has our seed money tied up in their own financial instruments sucking upward and circulating above the real economy within their **Cloud economy.**

Credit derivatives only represent a *claim* against, supposedly, real assets. When a financial instrument is a claim against another financial instrument (i.e. CDO Squared), what is its value as an asset? These financial instruments are **not** a real asset regardless of what financial institutions call them. In keeping with the spirit of Morgan-speak, they should be called *synthetic* assets.

Because Casino Capitalists are not investing in the real economy, Creation Capitalists cannot create real jobs. Capitalism has broken this clause of the Contract.

Upward mobility

One of the ways Capitalism avoids revolution and is allowed to accumulate wealth is through the concept of a classless society. Theoretically there are no barriers for one to rise upward in a Capitalist system.

(All right, I am aware of racism and women issues as regards capitalism. But let me continue with my assumption). If one has a brilliant idea, a brilliant product and is willing to sacrifice and work hard, there are no limitations on what that person can achieve. We have read numerous success stories of 'Joe Immigrant came here with only a nickel in his pocket and built a financial empire.' Or 'Billy Bebop came from the poorest family in PigStye Appalachia. Yet his dreams of building a company to (fill in the blank) came true.'

Upward mobility also means a rising standard of living (remember the tide and boats?). Without the Casino Capitalists investing in Creation Capitalism, there is no rising standard of living. And without money, dreams and brilliant ideas remain just that. The Casino Capitalists are not putting money towards the creation of new opportunities. Therefore, upward mobility is stagnant. In truth many are sliding backwards and the rest of us are holding on with our finger nails.

Another clause broken.

Stability

Every society needs, and demands stability. Society will even choose to continue bad governments over the fear of instability wrought through drastic change.

That is, until a significant percentage become No-Bread-ers. (Pay heed, Casino Capitalists). The stability of endless recession or depression is not an option. Look what happened to the Soviet Union.

Part of the Capitalist's Contract is to provide economic stability. Their enormous influence within our political system has been allowed as the price to control economic swings. The Federal Reserve was strongly endorsed by JP Morgan, the man. The economic panic of 1907 brought the banking system near collapse. Only Morgan's influence, money and efforts brought enough bankers together to arrest the financial fall. Morgan was so shaken by this 'near-miss,' he began the campaign, not to institutionalize Federal control over the economy, but to have a government reserve that could be tapped by bankers during times of economic stress. (Didn't quite work out that way, JP).

Even with the Fed controlling our money (or because of it) the stock market gyrates wildly. The dollar has crashed as measured against other currencies and gold. The economy has tanked and unemployment will not budge. Inflation is rearing its ugly head. (Don't believe Government statistics on inflation. Anyone that has bought groceries this year or taken the family out for a meal knows the inflation numbers are manipulated lies). This is the antithesis of stability.

Creation Capitalists detest instability. It ravishes everything: marketing plans, research & development, increased production, inventory expansion, introduction of new products, hiring of new employees and profits. In short, it throws everything on hold.

Casino Capitalists get a thrill out of instability. They call it *volatility*. This is the swing in prices (valuations) of financial instruments. It is a key component within their algorithms. It's how they make BIG money. Guess a market's going up and it does, they make money (going *long*). Guess the market's going down and it does, they make money (going *short*). They can win even when the economy tanks and the dollar falls! Hedge funds do it every day. These funds helped Lehman and Bear-Stearns stock fall right through the floor. The Hedge funds smelled blood in the water and short-sold every stock certificate of these two companies they could get their teeth into. (Sharks are such a group of swell guys).

And here is their dirty little secret never discussed in public; this is their *RUSH*. Victory through betting the correct market move is 'high-fived,' hooped and hollered behind trading doors; toasted over martini lunches. Stars are born, winning more money in one day than most small businesses make in five years.

You can't make this kind of bread in a stable market. Not enough volatility, Baby!

It happens in a day, an hour, a minute. That's why trading floors are so frantic and everyone is yelling. Billions of dollars are at stake. *Tic's* flying across digital screens are stared at harder than a picture of Mila Kunis in the buff (that's a compliment, Ms. Kunis. I have never seen a picture of you in the buff). Money is their aphrodisiac, not sex. Twenty and thirty year-old sharks are given keys to the vault and exhorted to go make money. If they win, the compensation is riches beyond any of our dreams. If they lose, they are branded 'rogue traders,' banished from the land of quick-money and, if losses are significant enough, chopped into sushi for an SEC lunch.

For the Casino Capitalists, every day is the highest-stakes crap game that anyone could ever play. *RUSH*, baby.

And it's all played with our nation's capital: bank deposits, pension plans, corporate profits, life insurance payments, home mortgages, medical plans, property tax payments, government tax payments, charitable trust funds, and even car and credit card debt (Personally, I don't mind if they lose that last one).

But the game is no fun if things are too stable. How many cries from Wall Street have you heard for spending cuts or balanced budgets? The silence is deafening. All the Casino Capitalists care about is the money supply. The last and current Secretaries of the Treasury are from two different political parties. But both are from The Street. Their solution to the economic collapse beginning in 2007: More money and more money. Never mind fixing what went wrong. Never mind curbing investment houses' excesses. Never mind demanding big financial changes in return for bail-outs. JUST LET US GET BACK TO THE GAMBLING TABLES!

Craps! We lose as a nation. Get out of the way and give the dice to the next thrower that has money in hand. Here comes Big Red (China). Let the games begin, again and again.

Volatility is their mantra and instability can bring our nation down. This clause of the Contract has been shattered.

Nationalism & patriotism

Capitalists have always rallied 'round the flag. For a free nation of law provides them:
- Political inclusion
- Legal protection
    Incorporation
    Right of contract
    Right of physical ownership
    Right of Intellectual Property ownership
    Right of bankruptcy
    Right of Corporate structure
    Right of intrastate & international trade

- Physical protection
    From international confiscation and attack
    From Citizenry theft
- Free international trade
- Beneficial Domestic Trade barriers
- Private ownership of natural resources
- Energy infrastructure for production of goods
- Transportation Infrastructure for transport of goods
- Labor
- Domestic markets

Quite a list of benefits. It only makes sense that Capitalists would revere and protect such a haven. But something changed the Casino Capitalists' loyalties. It was two major events: World War II and the advent of the digital age.

During World War II, larger corporations geared up for war-time production. The scale was exponential. And it required a visit to the Casino Capitalists, who demanded a trade: their kind of people in charge in exchange for their money. Leadership roles were occupied by money people instead of marketing and new products people. The largest corporations became extensions of the Casino Capitalists. Casino Capitalists not only received great returns on their investment, they also gained access to the largest corporate profits (and pensions) as part of their investment portfolios.

After World War II, manufacturing capabilities throughout the world had been either destroyed or worn out, except in America. Our nation alone was unscathed and newly tooled-up. It was an obvious move for large American corporations to fill the void and expand worldwide. It was the birth of the multi-nationals.

The second event was the digital explosion. Computerization and the internet made communication and information-sharing instantaneous. The multi-nationals could now run 24/7 without delays, from anywhere. Cyberspace made national borders irrelevant.

A natural evolution of the digital explosion was electronic trading. Again, 24/7 became the mantra and national borders became not only irrelevant, but a deterrent to the 'free-flow' of funds.   Casino Capitalists do not care if they deal in dollars, Euros, Rubles or Yuan. In actuality, they make money from derivatives that transfer capital from one currency to another.

The Casino Capitalists and Multi-nationals needed one other element: a level playing field. They brought American governmental influence, pressure and even military threat to bear upon other nations in order to 'homogenize' the world's business laws, trade laws, money laws, contract laws, custom fees, communications and market access. (Is it any wonder why so many peoples of different cultures hate us?)

They deemed this 'Free Trade.' However, it wasn't exactly 'free.' It cost a lot of blood and treasure.

The U.S. government has been so successful in this homogenization that the multi-nationals and the Casino Capitalists have become untethered to the nation that birthed them. The Casino Capitalists move our nation's capital to other countries to attain higher returns from even higher-risk investments. (Any time you invest in someone else's backyard, it's extremely risky, especially when they've sworn to destroy your country. That's one of the reasons they claim no nation). Multi-national corporations move jobs and manufacturing overseas for increased profits and access to larger markets.

Look at the economic rise of China. Once our mortal enemy, the multi-nationals and the Casino Capitalists have since fallen over each other in the rush to transfer America's wealth and America's future to the former 'Reds.' (Hey, boys and girls, they're still Communists). And, most sadly, China is one of our largest creditors. The Chinese must be shaking their heads at such disloyalty to a country, or laughing up their Mandarin sleeves. If the Multi-nationals and Casino Capitalists were Chinese, they would have been beheaded or sent to reeducation camps. (Hmmm, not a bad idea....no, that's childish). Actually, American's might have the last laugh if we default on our debt. Then, maybe the Chinese will include some of our government leaders in those beheadings. They should televise it. The ratings would be a killer...in both countries.

Casino Capitalists and their spawn, Multi-nationals, only drape themselves in our flag when their overseas assets are threatened or they smell fresh meat (profits) to pounce on (like Iraq's oil). They do not consider themselves fettered by such trite terms as nationalism and patriotism. They are above such bourgeois concerns. Their allegiance is to the nation of profits. The U.S. is just one of their markets and, increasingly, not their favorite.

The Loyalty Clause of the Capitalist Contract has been shredded.

Reinvestment in Creation Capitalism

Casino Capitalists are not reinvesting in American Creation Capitalism. The return is too boring. They would rather invest our national capital in the **Cloud economy** of high-risk financial instruments. They would rather invest our nation's capital in other nations.

Their arrogance, their disloyalty to our nation and its people, their risk-taking with our nation's capital stems from a dichotomy: they can invest our capital as they see fit because it's under their control, BUT, if they lose it, oh well, it wasn't their money anyway.

The Worst Theft

Remember the baby sharks swimming out of the Ivy Leagues. Well this is the worst crime that the Casino boys have perpetrated. They are stealing our best and brightest and putting these brilliant minds to work against us. Students that would have been aeronautical engineers instead develop programs that allow the Casino Capitalists to stretch the 'envelope' of maximum risk. Talented managers that could run our companies are tasked with driving sales crews to pawn off worthless financial instruments upon clueless customers. Mathematicians that could drive developments of new industries and keep the U.S. at the forefront of science are used to develop formulas predicting volatility and, hence, wild swings in markets.

Definitely this youth core is responsible for their own decisions. But if you had your nose to the grindstone for four years (plus advanced degrees) and you were in your twenties, a big fat paycheck out-of-the-shoot looks pretty inviting. We really can't blame our youth. It's our fault that we've allowed Wall Street to develop this aura of power, money and success so alluring to the young.

The financial 'industry' is a growing sector. In 1960, this industry represented less than 4% of our GDP. In 2008 it represented 8%. That's a HUNDRED PERCENT growth! (*Has the finance industry become less efficient?,* Thomas Phillipon, Stern School of Business, NYU, 2008)

I hate the term *industry* being applied to these people. Industry means creation of something worthwhile to society. All these jokers create is mayhem. And I am not interested in comments that this sector's growth is just a *natural* by-product of a growing economy. During the 1960's, a time of great economic growth for our nation, the financial sector's growth was nearly flat.

If you have any question as to why the financial sector has become so enticing to the cream of our educated youth, read these facts:

From 1973 to 1985, the financial sector never earned more than 16 percent of domestic corporate profits. In 1986, that figure reached 19 percent. In the 1990s, it oscillated between 21 percent and 30 percent, higher than it had ever been in the postwar period. This decade, it reached 41 percent. Pay rose just as dramatically. From 1948 to 1982, average compensation in the financial sector ranged between 99 percent and 108 percent of the average for all domestic private industries. From 1983, it shot upward, reaching 181 percent in 2007. (The Silent Coup, Simon Johnson, the Atlantic, May 2009).

Sounds like the sort of place I'd want to be, especially if I had $100k in student loans to pay off. What other industry can compete with those numbers? The Casino Capitalists are using our nation's capital and our nation's youth to slit our own throats.

I'm embarrassed.

The Big Drain

Know what's going to happen real soon? Well, that
Insatiable Cloud is going to drain.

Whoosh!

You might ask: *Isn't this a good thing?* Nope. Here's
why. I predict our economy will begin to tick-up
during 2012. And along with it, stock prices and
profits will become too enticing to the Casino boys.
They'll want in on the ride. So they're going to sell off
a BIG portion of their **Cloud economy** and invest it
into the real economy.

Well, isn't that what we want?

No. I am talking about TRILLIONS of dollars
tumbling down from the ethers into the economy here
on *terra firma* right at the time we don't need it. The
bankrolls of Casino Capitalists will cause the same
old problems; too much money chasing too few
resources…all on margin. Price/Earnings ratios of
companies' stocks will soar. And a huge credit
bubble will form, just waiting for the Federal Reserve
to raise interest rates in order to pop it.

Sure, the Casino Capitalists finally put the money
where we wanted it. But they did it at exactly the
wrong time. It's going to make the 1929 Crash look
like a one-day blip on the *Dow-Jones*.

Naturally, the smart boys will get out before the collapse, returning our capital back to the **Cloud**. And the ones caught with their pants down will go wailing to Washington that they're too big to fail. They will plead for their bail-outs, again.

And they'll get it. And the cycle will start all over.

Remember this, Money is a little bit different than the second law of thermodynamics (energy can neither be created nor destroyed). Money *can* be created. Just turn on a printing press. But it *can't* be destroyed. Whatever we print will be out there forever (or until the world doesn't honor it anymore).

The next bail out will be added to those already made. The sum is accumulative. And it's going to cause some real nasty inflation. I'm talking the BILLION Dollar note, instead of the Billion Deutsch Mark.

Better buy your wheelbarrow now.

The Score

So, late in the game, sports fans, here's the score:

**America & Creation Capitalists:
Zero**

**Casino Capitalists and their spawn:
All of our seed money**

PART III

PUNISHMENT PHASE

When the next BIG (and, boy do I mean BIG!) credit bubble bursts, Casino Capitalists are not only going to destroy themselves, they are taking down our dollar, our economy, the entire capitalist system, and our democracy. Washington, pay heed to that last point. If Democracy goes, so do you.

How do we stop these purveyors of mayhem before it's too late?

There are people who have tried. But it doesn't look good for a positive outcome. Four names have laid out their lines, trying to hook those big sharks on Wall Street.

Can You Say *Sarbanes-Oxley, Dodd-Franks?*

Quick, say the names ten times with a mouthful of marbles. Just kidding.

But these gentlemen weren't. In 2002, Senators Sarbanes & Oxley tried to reign in the deceit and fraud discovered within the Enron collapse. Off-shore, 'ghost' corporations hiding losses incurred right here at home were this energy company's big secret; until the music stopped and the coffers were empty and the Board of Directors ran for the hills (literally).

In response, *Sarbanes-Oxley* became law. It mandates that the top officers of public corporations (CEO's or CFO's or Presidents of corporations, whomever the spinning bottle stops on) sign and certify their year-end financial statements. This turns fantasy statements into more than a tall tale. It makes it a real crime with real jail time to falsify such statements.

Miraculously, there has been not ONE SINGLE prosecution of an officer of a financial institution since the industry's collapse in 2007. Either everything has been just bad luck or everyone else developed amnesia. That includes *Lehman, Citigroup, Countrywide*, even *AIG*.

Gee Whiz, I guess the boys that started the collapse that nearly brought down the world's financial system had absolutely no clue as to why their financial statements smelled like back bay water on a ninety-degree day.

Right.

Okay, who's sitting down on the job? Well, it's the SEC – Securities and Exchange Commission. It was created in 1934 in response to the '29 Wall Street crash. And interestingly, a savvy President Roosevelt put a fox in charge of the hen house. He appointed Joe Kennedy, one of the big Wall Street sharks. A man smart enough to see the crash was coming and short-sold stocks (betting they would go down). He was able to tell Congress how the game was played and how it could be stopped (or at least slowed down). The result was the *Glass-Steagall* Act that split up the banks into either deposit/loan banking or investment. The Casino Capitalists howled. Yet things worked pretty well for nearly forty years.

Until Congress began chipping away at *Glass-Steagall*, finally repealing it.

Today, the SEC continues to reach out-of-court settlements with the banks that caused the 2007 debacle. But no one goes to jail. I'm sure the banks see these settlements as just a cost of doing business. They'll make it up during the next game. The SEC says it's hard to convict someone of fraud, to show someone lied about numbers on their financials. Yet if this is true, then why has the SEC not gone to Congress and asked for specific laws that will put the Casino Capitalists behind bars? After all, a mainstay of other crimes is that 'ignorance of the law is not an excuse.' And these guys sure weren't ignorant.

The SEC appears not to want to upset or offend Wall Street. Wonder Why? Well, try this on. In 2006, 219 SEC employees filed papers wherein they notified their employer they were leaving to 'assist' clients that had business before the SEC (meaning Casino Capitalists under investigation).

But why leave to help the enemy? MONEY! The average salary of SEC lawyers is $100k to $195K. SEC examiners make between $90K and $160k. Sounds like big money. Most of us would be pretty satisfied with that salary (and a government pension, health care and other bene's).

Stack these numbers up against MILLIONS the banks can offer to make a problem go away. Why toil for twenty years when you can make the same in two-to-five?

Starting to get the picture? It's not lack of evidence that stalls the SEC. It's lack of conviction (literally).

I know one thing. Jack McCoy and the *Law and Order* gang wouldn't have needed a whole hour to tie up this episode. There has to be more evidence than a stained dress. Yet no one in Washington D. C. is making a sound.

Curiouser and curiouser, Holmes.

Dodd-Franks (the Banking Bill of 2009)

I'm not going to put you through the labyrinth and arcane-ness of our nation's capital. Let me just say this about Mr. Dodd and Mr. Frank's bill. They tried. They really did! It even addresses some of the issues I've covered in this book. However it got watered down. There are holes in the final bill that my 84 year-old mother could drive her Volvo through. (I have to pull her car into the garage. Either that or have my carpenter and masonry tools handy).

Let me give you just one of many examples:

First, it creates a commission (surprise!). It's called THE FINANCIAL STABILITY OVERSIGHT COUNCIL. Sounds *impressive*. Let's see who's on it:

> *the Secretary of the Treasury, who shall serve as Chairperson of the Council; the Chairman of the Board of Governors; the Comptroller of the Currency; the Director of the Bureau; the Chairman of the Commission; the Chairperson of the Corporation; the Chairperson of the Commodity Futures Trading Commission; the Director of the Federal Housing Finance Agency; the Chairman of the National Credit Union Administration Board; and an independent member appointed by the President.*

The gang's all here! All Federal, money agencies; the same ones that were on duty in 2007. The only difference is they can get together in public now. No more of those late-night, clandestine meetings as before that really put a hole in one's nocturnal cycle.

But wait, there's more. These persons are included as well:

> the Director of the Office of Financial Research; the Director of the Federal Insurance Office; a State insurance commissioner, to be designated by a selection process determined by the State insurance commissioners; a State banking supervisor, to be designated by a selection process determined by the State banking supervisors; and a State securities commissioner (or an officer performing like functions), to be designated by a selection

process determined by such State securities commissioners.

I'm not wild about the *Financial Research* or *Federal Insurance* offices. After all, they were around in 2007 as well. But bringing in the States is a little heartening. Maybe they can bring some enlightenment to this crowd and be the whistle blowers when our national economy appears to be going south.

But, alas, poor Yorick doesn't get a say. Just as with Shakespeare's non-speaking skull, this group of members is 'non-voting.'

Sigh.

Trying not to rain on Congress's parade, let's see what these boys get to do. Here's there main impetus:

> "...to identify risks to the financial stability of the United States that could arise from the material financial distress or failure, or ongoing activities, of large, interconnected bank holding companies or nonbank financial companies, or that could arise outside the financial services marketplace."

Maybe I'm a little slow, but isn't this the primary function of the Federal Reserve and department of Treasury? I'm pretty sure it is. So now we have a new commission to do what these boys were supposed to be doing before. That must mean they didn't do their jobs. So why has Tim Geithner and Ben Bernanke not been FIRED!

By now I think the American public has come to understand that when the Federal government creates a permanent commission, four things are true: 1) a big problem occurred, 2) no top guns will get fired, 3) the fallout will somehow be spread around a greater number of people, obfuscating who's to blame, and 4) the problem will occur again.

We shouldn't really get upset or spend time arguing about this bill, because it will not make any difference in the future.

And let me tell you why.

First, it is filled with more adjectives and adverbs than a Michener novel. 'stringent,' 'recommended,' 'in general,' 'may include,' 'prudential,' 'should be'; these are but a few plucked from a hundred. The importance is that they provide the wiggle room for *interpretation.* Any good Casino Capitalist (with the advice of his newly-hired SEC sidekick) will pluck this apart in court, or in hearings. Even if complicit, the old fallback, 'I wasn't aware' or 'I didn't realize,' or 'I didn't interpret it this way' or 'I was in the john trying to get that pesky paper off the end of the roll' will be used successfully to escape jail.

Second, only 13% of this law has been implemented since it was passed (*Boston Review*, August 2011). This bill is really not a law. It is a game plan that leaves it up to others to legally implement. Think the 'others' could be dragging their feet?

Naw.

And third, this law will be amended, watered down or repealed very soon. Why? Because Wall Street is loading up Congress with people who think Wall Street is the true center of Capitalism. Here are two facts to keep in mind: the Supreme Court has ruled that corporations (of which banks are corporations) can make political donations *without limits.* Banks have the money, so they're going to buy politicians and lobbyists that do their bidding. And their bidding means getting rid of this bill. In the last 10 years, Wall Street has contributed $5 BILLION to political campaigns and lobbyists (*Sold Out,* Center for Responsive Politics, www.opensecrets.org). Where do you think this number will go now that there are no legal restraints upon these institutions?

Ask and it shall be done. Casino Capitalists will ask the politicians and the bill will go bye-bye.

What Now?

It doesn't appear that Washington D.C. is the best place to hobble the Casino Capitalists. Remember, it's Washington that keeps refueling Wall Street's *Insatiable Cloud* economy. And who do you think is providing the insider information to all those Congressmen that are making hay while their terms last?

The answer lay with the States. Their politicians are closer to their people. The electorate can actually approach a State politician (and get him in a bear hug until he listens). These legislators can be swayed, pressured, pummeled (whatever is required) easier than assembling a thousand protestors in Washington D.C. Additionally, most State politicians would love to have the reputation of trimming the banks' sails, of forcing capital to be put to proper use in their State, of crowing over the number of new jobs created.

And if the State Capitol-ites don't listen, there is always the Initiative or Petition system. Most States have one. That should make financial institutions shudder, especially when you read later what I've got up my sleeve.

Here is the *real* weapon handed the States. It's the BIGGEST concession to States Rights in our nation's history. It's called *Cuomo v. Clearing House Association*. This incredible ruling by the U.S. Supreme Court in 2008 says that Federal law, as it relates to financial institutions, **DOES NOT** trump State law.

WOW! What a hammer. Now we need to find our *Thors* at the State level to swing it.

Here are the areas where laws need to be passed in order to rein-in Casino Capitalists, move the funding back to our Creation Capitalists and start really growing this economy again.

Credit derivatives & derivatives of Credit derivatives are Out!

Credit derivatives are **NOT** an asset, no matter what side of the balance sheet they occupy. They are not really a *claim* on an asset. They are a claim on the *debt* of an asset. To expand these derivatives by creating another derivative of them is insane. The so-called claim on the asset becomes obscure, and the original asset is not even identifiable. And the credit upon which they are bought creates an exponential increase to an already-bloated money supply. Casino Capitalists pig-out on our national capital, while starving out the Creation Capitalists. These are phantom financial instruments that have no real value; are not subject to understanding or scrutiny; and are ticking time bombs of economic destruction.

And, just to be clear, a derivative of a loan is a derivative of a derivative. The loan itself is a derivative because it *derives* its value from its claim upon an asset. This logic (and, hopefully, law) would kill CDS's, CDO's and CMO's. The dragon is slayed.

No New Financial Instruments!

Who gave Wall Street (or any Street) the right to create financial instruments? The term *innovation* should apply to new products or new services, not our financial instruments. The way Casino Capitalists use the term, *innovation* means obfuscation, legal circumvention, high-stakes gambling and a well-disguised con job. We need old-fashioned, staid, mundane, understandable, predictable instruments that have been around for generations. We need stability.

Make it instantly illegal for anyone to create a new financial instrument without, first, public hearings, governmental scrutiny and a follow-on vote. There should be some overriding benefit to the nation for this instrument to exist in the first place. Any whacky, self-serving idea Wall Street comes up with must be the subject of *extensive* public hearings, *have* the approval of the appropriate State regulatory commission, a TWO-THIRDS majority vote in both houses of the State's legislative system and the Governor's signature. Then there should be a five-year test period with the sponsoring financial institution only. Then more public hearings and a regulatory commission opinion on the instruments financial impact reported to the legislature. Then hold another legislative vote (requiring a two-thirds majority) along with another signature of the Governor.

My gosh, it sounds almost impossible to get a new financial instrument approved!

Yes, it does, doesn't it?

No Bundling within credit derivatives

Any bundling, by definition, creates a derivative. Kill bundling and we kill derivatives because the main attraction of derivatives is that they, supposedly, represent diversity within a single investment. Well, a hurricane has a lot of diversity packed into its Category 5 winds. But it also does a lot of damage. No one can expect to know the individual credit ratings or worthiness of 1000 loans represented by a single financial instrument (even when a rating agency rubber stamps it with AAA).

No bundling, period.

Split the Deck

Okay, you Casino Capitalists, we know you don't play well with other kids. So we're splitting you up.

The States need to bring back their version of the *Glass-Steagall Act*. Well, in truth they would have to call it the *Frankenstein of Glass-Steagall* because it goes a lot farther than the original.

Here's how it would lay out:

Create four levels of licensing and regulation for private banks: **Retail, Commercial, Investment** and **Speculative.** Participation at each level would be based upon 'tiered' deposits. This means, to bank at a certain level you have to maintain a certain deposit level at each stage underneath you. We do not want Citizens investing their life savings in high risk securities. You can shout 'It's their money!' But who do the losers come running to when the games end, they lose all their money and they're about to lose their home? US! I don't know about you, but I'm getting a little tired of bailing out everyone's butt my own. No one offers to bail me out when I make a stupid investment (I know it's hard to believe, but I've made some beauties).

Tier one: Retail banking would include mortgages, consumer loans and tier-one deposits (Set at a level that demonstrates responsibility and the ability to manage money; indexed to keep up with inflation).When depositors achieved the minimum savings at this level; they are allowed to invest at the next level.

Tier-two: Commercial. Corporations start at this level. The rate of return on savings for investors is higher. Additionally, they offer financial investments of equities and bonds considered conservative and 'safe' (as established by commission regulations). If the individual has the required savings and/or investments in tier two, they can move to the next level.

Tier three: Investment banking. Every State commission-approved financial instrument is available at this level. Pension funds and government agencies can invest at this level. The required assets to move up from here would put any person in the 'mega-rich' category.

Tier-four: speculative banking. No banks, publicly-traded companies, pension funds, insurance companies or government agencies can invest at this level. Speculative banks would be a combination of a Wall-Street investment bank, hedge fund, arbitrage and international financier. They can do all the gambling they want at this level, but not with the majority of our nation's capital. These banks would have limits too. They would only be funded by wealthy individuals, privately-held corporations or loans from other speculative banks. And there would be a maximum that each investor could have within each speculative bank and a cap set on the total assets the bank controlled. The investment amount and total assets should be constrained in the millions, not billions. That way, if one goes belly-up (like Long Term Capital Management), it doesn't threaten our entire financial system.

Here are some other sphincter-tightening rules: Banks below 'speculative' can only loan to other banks that are incorporated within that State. NO LOANS TO OUT-OF-STATE BANKS. NO LOANS TO OTHER COUNTRIES. We're selfish. We want our national capital to be loaned within our State, our country. Our Federal government already blows enough of our money on other nations. Just check how much they put into the IMF – International Monetary Fund.

Additionally, NO BANK CAN LOAN TO ANOTHER BANK OUTSIDE ITS TIER. What this means is that a retail bank cannot put money into an investment bank. We want it to invest in our Citizens, not in risky financial instruments. A bank can loan to another bank within its tier. But there should be a cap on the total amount loaned in this manner, and a cap on the loan amount to any individual bank.

Set leverage limits for banks at all levels. The lower the tier, the lower the leverage number. These should be really low. I personally believe anything above 5:1 is insane. But then, what do I know. I save my gambling for the once-a-year road trip to Vegas.

This is what tiered banking accomplishes:

Banks concentrate on loaning capital for use within the economy here on *terra firma* (not up in the **CLOUD economy**)

Banks have increasing capital reserves at each level in order to guarantee their solvency during times of economic stress.

Banks representing *Main Street's* money do not invest in high-risk instruments.

Banks are forced to invest in Creation Capitalists (who create real wealth, real assets, and real jobs)

Bankers are retrained to serve their original values: conservative investments; protection of deposits; long range financial stability of the bank.

Banks of the same tier are on a level playing field with each other. There is no pressure to compete with risky investments against another bank reaching for the quick buck.

Casino Capitalists are rounded up and corralled within speculative banking where they can only get their hands on hundreds of millions, not billions of our national capital.

<u>Unbelievable! They Actually Get Away With This!</u>

Here are the main areas within which financial institutions love to stretch the moral envelope. To those of us not steeped in the financial jargon, these points can seem a little arcane. But, believe me, they are important to control. These Casino Capitalists have to be reined-in with tough rules that leave no ambiguities or 'wiggle' room:

Ratings Agencies: Believe it or not, ratings for derivative bonds were rubber stamped by Moody's and Standard & Poor. (I know, hard to believe). These rating giants did not do their job and should not be trusted in the future. Empower a State agency that uses a standard, cast-in-stone algorithm to evaluate risk of financial instruments and produce a one-to-four rating.   It is not that complicated and it is done all the time by banks when evaluating potential loans. If you run a business and want a loan, banks 'crunch' your financials through many different 'ratios' in order to determine your credit worthiness. Take those ratios and apply them to a financial instrument. Then 'weight' each ratio and produce a rating. Not that hard, really. The reason investment banks have complex, super-computer crunching programs for risk scenarios that are beyond the NSA's encryption codes is that the financial instruments they are buying and selling actually have no known worth. Their only worth is what they can peddle them for, that day; that minute. (It's called the 'tea-leaves' method). So what they are actually tracking is how far they can get to the edge of some so-called risk curve without collapsing the company. They only assess risk of trade, not risk of instrument. Triple 'A' ratings on derivative bonds were just a formality to let the games begin. They had absolutely no relationship as to what was within the bonds.

Evaluation of a financial instrument's worth should be based solely on its intrinsic value; the value of the assets it directly represents. This is the only rating that should matter.

Clearing Houses: Again, another 'believe-it-or-not.' Investment houses do not use independent clearing houses for their high-risk instruments. They are traded directly from buyer to seller. This has staggering implications in areas of fraud as well as financial collapse due to inability of settlement. There is legislation pending to cover this, but to date it still languishes. If, as I propose, a new instrument has to be approved over time and through State legislatures before it can be traded, then these legislatures should demand a clearing house be assigned these instruments from the get go.

Market to Market Evaluations Only: (I'll stop with the 'unbelievable' because it all is). When everything collapsed in 2007~2008, the SEC (with encouragement from the Fed) allowed banks to value their worthless derivatives at what they paid for them. If they were valued at what they could be sold for, nearly all of our major financial institutions would have been declared insolvent. The reason: no one was buying the garbage, so the garbage was worthless (actually, that's an insult to garbage, because it has a per-ton price). The scary part is that billions of dollars of these 'toxic' assets are still on the banks' books. It will take decades to flush all this out, assuming we don't add anymore (which they are doing even as you read this). If there were an established trading floor for these instruments, there would be a 'Bid' and 'Ask' each day, and this would be the valuation for the products. This is market-to-market valuation and should be the only one allowed.

If you or I pledge publically-traded stock as collateral for a loan, do you think the bank would assess our daily credit worthiness on what we paid for the stock? Hell….ah, sorry, Heck no! Its only value is the market price today, this minute. So why are banks allowed to name their own price for pieces of paper they deem 'assets'?

Oh yeah, they directly access the money's printer, our Federal government.

No Off-Books, No Off-Shore: Legal actions still hound the Enron guys that tried these tricks: take bad assets off the books and park them off-shore so stock holders won't know how really bad things are.

Yet banks do it every day. And the government agencies that are supposed to control these financial paragons sanction the parlor tricks. If you really don't think Washington and Wall Street dance hand-in-hand, this one point should rock your foundation.

If we would not allow a publically-traded corporation to use fraudulent accounting methods, then why in the Bejesus would we allow our banks? STOP IT, NOW!

No Margin Trading: trading on margin is when the buyer puts only a portion of the money down to purchase a financial instrument. It is usually twenty percent. And this is credit. It allows the buyer to control 100% of an asset while only paying 20%. This means that for every dollar of investment, the buyer controls five times that amount.

This practice, this credit extension needs to end, for all equities: bonds and stocks.

But what's the problem with this? Isn't this good for investing in America?

Absolutely not. True 'investing' implies buying something with OTHER PEOPLE'S MONEY. Margin means buying it with OUR money (our national capital). Anytime someone doesn't pay a hundred percent for something, the seller is gambling that you can eventually pay it off. This is gambling. We can understand this credit extension on a real asset (i.e. a house). But not on something that has a minute-to-minute value fluctuation. This is pure gambling. Anyone involved needs to float it on their money, not ours.

Margin credit (like any credit) expands the money supply. When you can buy five times what you can afford, it doesn't matter if it is a stock certificate or a derivative bond. Prices go up from this inflationary pressure. Stocks trade for multiples of earnings that become unrealistic. If there is a lot of money pumped into the economy (like now), it will eventually create a credit bubble that will burst along with financial markets. It's 1929 all over again. And for what?

Does margin buying increase real economic activity? Perhaps. If a company uses its stock as collateral for loans to increase production capabilities or to increase inventories, economic activity is positively impacted. But when the bubble bursts and new business dries up, what happens to the increased capacity, the increased inventories? They become an albatross to the company, along with the incurred loans to pay for them. The resulting recession is deepened and lengthened as companies eat slowly through inventories while idling production. And idled production translates into lost jobs.

I ask again, what is the purpose of margin buying? The answer: it's a way to sell more product. And that product is financial instruments. We inflate our companies' stock prices and overheat our economy so that Casino Capitalists can make more money from trades. Because this is the real reason for margin buying and selling: increased profits for Wall Street.

And, once again, the Casino Capitalists have risked our nation's capital for their personal gain. Here's the real risk created: the margin call. This occurs when the stock price falls more than the 20% originally invested. And the buyer must make good the difference. But the problem is the buyer doesn't have the reserve to cover it because he used all his money to leverage other stock purchases. The buyer dumps the stock, causing panic selling and further downward pressure on the market. If the buyer is out of funds, he defaults and the financial institution that extended the credit is on the hook for the accelerating drop in the stock's price. Quickly the financial institution faces insolvency because it cannot cover all these losses. And then we enjoy a nice long depression.

I'll say it again.

And for what: the production of huge profits for a small segment of players with a financial game that produces nothing but grief and misery for the rest of us?

STOP THIS SELLING ON MARGIN! Make the buyer come up with 100% of the stock price or don't be a buyer. If the market turns down, the buyer doesn't have to come up with additional funds (which he probably doesn't have). And, if he chooses, he can ride the stock down and wait for a turn around. If a majority of buyers did this, the downturn would be less and the duration would be less. Panic selling would be diminished and prices would stabilize quicker.

No Equity lines & No ARM's: This speaks to the equity lines on homes (secured by second-trust-deeds) and adjustable-rate-mortgages that financial institutions did (and still do) issue to home owners. There is no positive outcome for the individual or our society by allowing the existence of either instrument. Equity lines encourage home owners to use the equity in their homes to spend on consumables (cars, boats and vacations) saddling them with long range debt. If they encounter an economic shock (like losing their job), they cannot make the payments and the house joins the growing number of foreclosures. The real evil part of equity lines is that they are issued in the same way as credit cards: adjustable rates. These lines can be as expensive as Master Card debt. The homeowners that use these lines will be paying them off for decades. Most will not succeed in keeping up with increasing interest rates and will have to sell their home to escape the debt. Or they will just walk away leaving another foreclosure on the block.

ARMs are just plain evil. If a family cannot afford the monthly payment on a 30 year loan, mortgage brokers entice them into an ARM at a low interest rate. The problem is the rates go up dramatically within 5 years or when interest rates tick up. In the last financial debacle, many of these home owners faced increases in monthly payments of 500 to 1000% over their initial payments. And we all know how well that worked out. The entire residential construction industry has been idled (and will continue to be idled for years) because of all the excess inventory of homes on the market due to foreclosures.

Second-trust deeds can be a valuable tool for improving a property, expanding a house. If it is used for this purpose only, it should be allowed to exist. But laws should stipulate the extent of this use.

NO EQUITY LINES AND NO ARMS!

These boys and girls, the Casino Capitalists, have been misbehaving and we need to motivate them to pursue the righteous path; that of their origin and one that benefits us all. We want them to invest in our economy and stop staying out late, partying and, most of all, gambling (with our money!).

Defanging the Beast is a Taxing Problem

Another problem is our tax system. These boys and girls ruling over our nation's capital are taxed on their winnings at capital gains rates from 15 to 20%. A gambler winning the U.S. Poker Championship would have to declare his winnings as 'earned income' and pay somewhere around 45%. Now, gambling is gambling and this doesn't seem fair.

I am for the lowest capital gains tax society will accept. It's been proven over and over that reducing capital gains returns more capital to the economy to create more business and, hence, more jobs. But capital gains tax schedules were created to release capital from long-sitting assets: a building, land, even a business. It's a travesty (and counterproductive) to apply this to traders on Wall Street. Capital gains just feed the Casino Capitalist gambling habit by allowing them to turn over billions of dollars of stocks and bonds daily. Buy today, make a few shekels, sell it all and look for the next bet.

This turn-over kills planning of business leaders. If they plan long-term growth based on loans (which are, in turn, based on the company's stock price) it's an up and down, roller-coaster ride that forces Creation Capitalists to be short range. And short range means no growth. In some ways it can mean negative growth because the incentive becomes cost cutting, not expansion (fewer jobs rather than more).

Now, to apply capital gains rates to derivatives is just downright stupid. It's like shaking a fistful of dice in the ear of a reformed gambler. He starts to sweat. Then licks dry lips and finally finds himself on his knees in the back alley with the other boys, yelling 'Come on 7!'

Remember this one key point: WE DON'T WANT OUR NATION'S CAPITAL IN DERIVATIVES. So why in the heck are we encouraging this bad-boy habit through our tax laws?

The answer: redo capital gains laws for all financial instruments (stocks, bonds, derivatives) to reflect long-range commitment to growth. If you cash-in year one (or any time during that year), capital gains is 50%; second year, 40%; third year, 30%; fourth year, 20%; fifth year, 10%. And if you hold it five years and one day, ZERO PERCENT. That's right, no tax for five years of faith and commitment. (That beats a marriage commitment!). What does society get out of it? Economic stability of longer-range growth, more jobs, more research and development of new products and more national wealth.

Kill foreign investments

The other day I attended a Veterans' Day Assembly at the local elementary school. By the time it was over, I had tears streaming down my cheeks. Heck, I got choked up just saying the Pledge of Allegiance. I love America. I care about all Americans. I really don't care what's going on in China or Bangladesh unless it directly impacts my country.

I believe in investing our nation's capital within our nation.

HEY, SHORT-SIGHTED CASINO CAPITALISTS, IF YOU DON'T START INVESTING IN THE COUNTRY THAT CREATED THE WEALTH YOU ARE DESTROYING, START LOOKING OUT THROUGH THE FRONT DRAPES! That mob with the pitch forks and torches is there to explain how the new laws work. Of course you won't be hanging around long enough to see the effect. You'll just be hanging. You can remain arrogant and think the unwashed masses will continue to take it.

But remember what happened to Marie Antoinette right after she said, "Let them eat cake!" And none of your clan is as pretty as she was.

IF YOU CAN'T BE MOVED BY PATRIOTISM (A LOVE OF THE COUNTRY THAT MADE YOU RICH), THEN HOW ABOUT THE SELFISH INDUCEMENT OF SURVIVAL!

INVEST IN AMERICA, NOT IN FOREIGN COMPANIES OR COUNTRIES.

I am not advocating violence against anyone. I abhor it. I am just trying to point out that frustration with government, hopelessness and grinding poverty lead to revolution. And most revolutions focus on a specific foe and become quite violent.

There should be banking laws that stop the flight of our national capital outside our borders. This doesn't mean buying or selling, or the euphemistic term "free-trade" (I will address this in a future writing). It means investing outside our borders.

I know what will be yelled, "The free-flow of capital is the underpinning to Capitalism." Couldn't agree more. I just say let it free-flow here. If you Casino Capitalist are so in love with other countries, then go live there. No problem. Don't let the door hit you in the butt. Oh, but just one thing: leave our money here.

I'll leave it up to others trained in legalese to sort out the terms. But it better be written with no wiggle room.

WHAT GIVES US THE RIGHT?

Before we accomplish anything, it's going to get real ugly. Casino Capitalists and their bought-and-paid-for spokespersons (i.e. politicians, Federal Reserve Chairman and Secretary of the Treasury) will trot out the old, worn axioms and tirades against us: we're socialists; we will destroy Capitalism with our hair-brained laws; we have no right to abridge economic freedoms.

Here's our response:

First, we're not socialists. We're trying to make sure that our country *doesn't* go socialist. If we allow you Casino Capitalists to continue gambling (and losing) our nation's capital, people will begin to think Capitalism has failed. This is what the real socialists are waiting for; you to throw the door wide open. And we must stop you.

Second, we intend to save Capitalism; Creation Capitalism that is the backbone of this country. You are the ones that are destroying it. We're going to give you some new (and old) rules that you have to play by, or you can't play. You Casino Capitalists think you are the most important cog in the system; that our national wealth stems from you. You need a little reeducation. We just need the money you control to flow into our nation's investments, not into your crazy, made up investments. That's your job. If you cannot do it properly, you're fired! Get out. There are a hundred people ready to take your job. And we will make sure they understand the rules better.

Third, we have all right (moral, legal, biggest guy on the block, whatever) to control our nation's capital. You Casino Capitalists create absolutely NO wealth. You administer it, that's all. And you've done a poor job of that. Creation Capitalists, along with the people that work for them and their customers and vendors that complete the cycle; these are the ones that create ALL of our nation's wealth. The capital sitting in our financial institutions **is as much our nation's as it is the institution holding it**. Why? **Because those that say they own it, or control it, already lost it in 2007**. It was the American taxpayer, us, that came to the rescue and refilled their coffers when they were empty.   As we will be paying off this money for generations to come, yes, we feel we have some say-so in how it is administered. We're not talking about confiscation.

We leave that to the Socialists should you not heed our warnings.

'NO-BREAD-ERS,' LISTEN UP

I want to first say, thanks. I'm glad *someone* is focusing on the real perps. You are performing a valuable service for all Americans, and that is bringing attention to a serious problem that threatens our nation.

With that said, I have to turn a bit critical and say:

GET A COHESIVE, ACTION-DRIVEN MESSAGE OUT THERE!

You are right about Wall Street. Now you have to get specific not only with your criticisms but with a plan to fix things. And you must roll-in their Washington accomplices. It's a 'target rich' environment. Search this book for rallying cries. I offer my thoughts to help win this fight.

Remember this, Creation Capitalism built our wealth and can do so again. Don't throw out the baby with the bath water. Target your efforts upon the Casino Capitalists, the President and the Congress.

But the real solution is to galvanize action at the State level. Whether through State legislatures or an

Initiative or Petition system, take the remedies in this book and make them law. The Casino Capitalists own Washington. That is their focus and where they buy influence. If you start with the States, the Casino boys might be caught flat-footed.

Move fast before they can channel resources to blunt your efforts.

AND, MOST IMPORTANT, DO NOT...REPEAT....DO NOT BUY INTO THE SOCIALIST MESSAGE THAT CAPITALISM IS THE PROBLEM.

M.A. Farrell

www.firethefederalgovernment.com (books)

www.firethefederalgovernment.org (blog)